Why There is Bad, Where We Live....

A. J. CARICO

WestBow Press books may be ordered through booksellers or by contacting:

WestBow Press
A Division of Thomas Nelson & Zondervan
1663 Liberty Drive
Bloomington, IN 47403
www.westbowpress.com
844-714-3454

ISBN: 978-1-6642-8254-4 (sc)
ISBN: 978-1-6642-8253-7 (e)

Library of Congress Control Number: 2022920083

Print information available on the last page.

WestBow Press rev. date: 04/11/2023

This book is dedicated
to my beloved son, Jon,
who advised me to teach,
by writing a book.

Why There Is Bad
Where We Live….

Where we live is in the **Physical Realm**.

The Physical Realm is where we use our five senses: sight, touch, hearing, taste and smell. We see our houses, family and friends.

We hear birds singing.
We smell flowers.

We taste the birthday cake at parties.
And, we touch our video controllers and school books.

In the Physical Realm there is '**Good**'. Examples of good are: Telling the truth; Respecting our parents; Being kind to others; And, not stealing. Good people are friendly, kind, and wear a smile most of the time, but not always.

'**Bad**' exists in the Physical Realm, too. Bad is the opposite of good. Examples of bad are hitting, lying, stealing, saying and doing things that make others cry.

The Physical Realm is where we praise the **Lord God Almighty**, who lives in the Spiritual Realm.

In the **Spiritual Realm** are things we do not see, hear, feel, taste or smell. The Spiritual Realm is not like when we play pretend. The Spiritual Realm is real, just like the Physical Realm, but we cannot see it.

In the Spiritual Realm, God exists in the form of *The Holy Trinity*: God the Father; God, the Son (Jesus); and God, the Holy Spirit. (1 John 5:7 NKJV)[1] It is hard for us to understand The Holy Trinity: How God can be one and three different beings at the same time. That is because we live in the Physical Realm where one person can only be one person. But that is who God is, He can do anything. The Bible says, "All things are possible with God." (Matthew 19:26 NIV)[2] It also says, "All good things come from God." (James 1:17 NIV)[3]

God, the Father, being good, (Luke 18:19b NLT)[4] does not like bad.

God wants only good in Heaven with Him, His Son, Jesus and the Holy Spirit.

But, once a long, long time ago, there was bad in Heaven. One of the heavenly beings, decided to rebel against God, because he wanted some of what God had.

God won the battle over bad because He is the one and only true Sovereign God, who created the universe. (Genesis 1:1 NIV)[5] He is all powerful and all knowing. (2 Chronicles 20:6 NLT)[6] (Luke 12:7a NIV)[7]

God cannot tolerate bad, so He punished Satan by throwing him out of Heaven. "Then war broke out in heaven. Michael and his angels fought against the dragon, and the dragon and his angels fought back. But he was not strong enough, and they lost their place in heaven. The great dragon was hurled down—that ancient serpent called the devil, or Satan, who leads the whole world astray. He was hurled to the earth, and his angels with him." (Revelation 12:7-9 NIV) Jesus said, "I saw Satan fall like lightning from heaven." (Luke 10:18 NIV)

That is why there is good and bad in our Physical Realm today. All bad comes from Satan.

God gave Satan the punishment of residing for eternity in a terrible place referred to as "a lake of fire" (Revelation 19:20 KJV)[8], at the end of this age. Satan got so mad about it, he decided he would take as many humans with him into the lake of fire as he could. So, Satan tries every day to trick people to hate one another. Because if we hate, we will do bad things. The Bible says it is not people that are our problem, but Satan. (Ephesians 6:12 NIV)[9]

God, being loving and good, wants no one to be tricked by Satan. So God devised a solution to help everyone be good, so they could go live with Him in Heaven, forever.

The solution began in the Spiritual Realm, but it was finished in the Physical Realm.

God's solution to help everyone say and do good things, involves His Son, **Jesus and the Holy Spirit.** The Bible says, "For God so loved the world that he gave his one and only Son, that whoever believes in him shall not perish but have eternal life." (John 3:16 NIV) God resolved to send his Son, Jesus down from Heaven, to be born of a virgin, as a baby boy here on earth. That is why we celebrate the Christmas season. We remember Jesus' birth into the Physical Realm.

Jesus grew from a baby into a boy, became a teenager, and matured into a man. All this time, Jesus always did what was right. (1 Peter 2:22 NASB)[10]

When Jesus was a man, He went about performing miracles. He helped others by healing the sick and afflicted and feeding the hungry. Jesus walked on water and calmed a storm just by speaking to the wind and waves. (Mark 4:39 NKJV)[11] More importantly, Jesus forgave sins, raised the dead and taught about His good Father, God.

Jesus said about himself: "The Spirit of the Lord is upon Me, Because He has anointed Me To preach the gospel to the poor; He has sent Me to heal the brokenhearted, To proclaim liberty to the captives And recovery of sight to the blind, To set at liberty those who are oppressed; To proclaim the acceptable year of the Lord." (Luke 4:18-19 NKJV)

Jesus came to earth knowing his destiny. He was to be the perfect sacrifice for our sins because He was sinless. God's true assignment for Jesus in the Physical Realm, was to die on the cross to save us from our sins. (Romans 5:8 NKJV)[12]. Jesus died on a Friday, which we call 'Good Friday', because it was good for us.

When He died, Jesus paid the price (the Bible calls our sin debt, Colossians 2:14 NASB and Colossians 1:13-14 NASB)[13], for all of us not being good. He was buried in a tomb. God raised his Son from the dead on 'the third day'. (Luke 24:46 NIV)[14].

Nowadays on Resurrection Sunday, we celebrate Jesus Christ rising from the dead, victorious over sin and death.

Forty days after Jesus rose from the dead, He ascended back into Heaven, where He prepares a place for us.

So, how does this help us be good?

On the day of Pentecost, when the people learned Jesus, whom they had crucified, was the promised **Messiah** sent from God, they asked, "What shall we do?" The Bible says in Acts 2:38 (NIV), "Peter replied, 'Repent and be baptized, every one of you, in the name of Jesus Christ for the forgiveness of your sins. And you will receive the gift of the Holy Spirit.'"

The Holy Spirit, a part of **The Holy Trinity**, comes to live inside our hearts. The Holy Spirit is something like a Superhero, who helps us know the right thing to do and say, then, gives us strength to do and say it, as we serve God in the Physical Realm. The Holy Spirit is also called, "The Helper" (John 14:26 NKJV)[15], because he helps us to feel joy in our hearts, no matter the circumstances. The Holy Spirit gives us insight and good judgment to make right choices. The Bible says, the Holy Spirit even helps us pray, when we don't know what to say. (Romans 8:26-27 NIV)[16]

So when we choose to do good, we are honoring **God, the Father; God, the Son (Jesus); and God, the Holy Spirit.**

It is not always easy, because our enemy, Satan, makes a Christian's life more difficult. He does this to discourage us, to make us turn away from God. To help us hold on to our faith in Jesus, God promises in Romans 8:28 (NASB), "And we know that all things work together for good for those who love God, to those who are the called, according to His purpose." God promises when bad things happen to us, He will make good out of it, just because we love Jesus. There are many accounts of this in the Bible.

That is why when we believe God's Word, the Bible, and follow His teachings, Jesus will forgive our sins. Then, we can serve Him here in the Physical Realm until we go to live with Him for eternity in the Spiritual Realm. We show we accept Jesus as our Redeemer by confessing our sins and being baptized, attending Church regularly and partaking of Communion as given by example in the Bible. ("Now on the first day of the week, when the disciples came together to break bread, Paul... spoke to them and continued his message until midnight." Acts 20:7 NKJV) Because Jesus died to save us from our sins, we are given the opportunity to go to Heaven and live with Him forever. Life in Heaven will be perfect because only good is there." (Revelation 21:27 NIV)[17] It is written in the Bible: "...No eye has seen, no ear has heard, and no mind has imagined what God has prepared for those who love him." (1 Corinthians 2:9b NLT) And, "He (God) will wipe every tear from their eyes. There will be no more death or mourning or crying or pain, for the old order of things has passed." (Revelation 21:4 NIV)

The only way to get to Heaven is by accepting Jesus as our Savior and Lord. (John 14:6 NIV)[18]

The Bible says God waits patiently for everyone to choose Jesus as their Savior. (2 Peter 3:9 NIV)[19]

Will you choose good today?

Will you choose to accept Jesus as your Savior?

Will you choose to say you are sorry (repentant) for the things you have done wrong?

Will you choose to be baptized (immersed in water) in the name of the Father (God), the Son, (Jesus) and the Holy Spirit?

Will you choose to live a good life (raised to walk in a newness of life), telling others about how Jesus left his good life in Heaven, just to save us from our sins, so we can live a good life, too?

Talk to your Mom, Dad, Minister, or other grown up to arrange for the preparations for you to have a good life here on earth, where we live...

Notes

1 "For there are three that bear witness in heaven: the Father, the Word, and the Holy Spirit; and these three are one." (1 John 5:7 NKJV)

2 "Jesus looked at them and said, 'With man this is impossible, but with God all things are possible.'" (Matthew 19:26 NIV)

3 "Every good and perfect gift is from above, coming down from the Father of the heavenly lights, who does not change like shifting shadows." (James 1:17 NIV)

4 ..."Only God is truly good." (Luke 18:19b NLT)

5 "In the beginning God created the heavens and the earth." (Genesis 1:1 NIV)

6 "He prayed, O LORD, God of our ancestors, you alone are the God who is in heaven. You are ruler of all the kingdoms of the earth. You are powerful and mighty; no one can stand against you!" (2 Chronicles 20:6 NLT)

7 "Indeed, the very hairs of your head are all numbered..." (Luke 12:7a NIV)

8 "And the beast was taken, and with him the false prophet that wrought miracles before him, with which he deceived them that had received the mark of the beast, and them that worshiped his image. These both were cast alive into a lake of fire burning with brimstone." (Revelation 19:20 KJV)

9 "For our struggle is not against flesh and blood, but against the rulers, against the authorities, against the powers of this dark world, and against the spiritual forces of evil in the heavenly realms." (Ephesians 6:12 NIV)

10 "WHO COMMITED NO SIN, NOR WAS ANY DECEIT FOUND IN HIS MOUTH;" (1 Peter 2:22 NASB)

11 "...Peace, be still!" (Mark 4:39 NKJV)

12 "But God demonstrates His own love for us, in that while we were still sinners, Christ died for us." (Romans 5:8 NKJV)

13 ...,"having canceled out the certificate of debt consisting of decrees against us, which was hostile to us; and He has taken it out of the way, having nailed it to the cross." (Colossians 2:14 NASB) "For He rescued us from the domain of darkness, and transferred us into the kingdom of His beloved Son, in whom we have redemption, the forgiveness of sins." (Colossians 1:13-14 NASB)

14 ..."This is what is written: The Christ will suffer and rise from the dead on the third day,"... (Luke 24:46b NIV)

15 "But the Helper, the Holy Spirit, whom my Father will send in My name, He will teach you all things, and bring all things to your remembrance, all things that I said to you." (John 14:26 NKJV)

16 "In the same way, the Spirit helps us in our weakness. We do not know what we ought to pray for, but the Spirit himself intercedes for us with groans that words cannot express. And he who searches our hearts knows the mind of the Spirit, because the Spirit intercedes for the saints in accordance with God's will." (Romans 8:26-27 NIV)

17 "Nothing impure will ever enter it, nor will anyone who does what is shameful or deceitful, but only those names are written in the Lamb's book of life." (Revelation 21:27 NIV)

18 "Jesus answered, 'I am the way and the truth and the life. No one comes to the Father except through me.'" (John 14:6 NIV)

19 "The Lord is not slow in keeping his promise, as some understand slowness. He is patient with you, not wanting anyone to perish, but everyone to come to repentance." (2 Peter 3:9 NIV)

Printed in the United States
by Baker & Taylor Publisher Services